Cher

Julia Holt

Published in association with The Basic Skills Agency

Hodder & Stoughton

A MEMBER OF THE HODDER HEADLINE GROUP

Acknowledgements
Cover: Neil Mums/PA Photos

Photos: pp 8, 27 © Retna; p 10 © Corbis; pp 14, 17, 25 © All Action; pp 20 © Warner Bros/The Ronald Grant Archive; p22 © Orion/Rank/The Ronald Grant Archive

Orders: please contact Bookpoint Ltd, 39 Milton Park, Abingdon, Oxon OX14 4SB. Telephone (44) 01235 827720, Fax: (44) 01235 400454. lines are open from 9.00–6.00, Monday to Saturday, with a 24 hour message answering service. You can also order through our website www.hodderheadline.co.uk

British Library Cataloguing in Publication Data
A catalogue record for this title is available from the British Library

ISBN 0 340 80093 3

First published 2001
Impression number   10 9 8 7 6 5 4 3 2
Year   2007 2006 2005 2004

Copyright © 2001 Julia Holt

Typeset by SX Composing DTP, Rayleigh, Essex
Printed in Great Britain for Hodder & Stoughton Educational, a division of Hodder Headline 338 Euston Road, London NW1 3BH by CPI Bath

Contents

1 Introduction

Cher is a survivor.
She has survived for forty years
in the worlds of music and film.
These are worlds
that forget people very quickly.
But not her.
She is a superstar.

Cher has also survived
a very difficult childhood.
Every time her mother married,
the family moved house
and Cher moved school.
Her beautiful mother
sometimes had small parts in films.
Sometimes they had money
but most of the time they didn't.

2   Early Life

Cher was born on 20 May 1946
in a small town in California.
By the time she was born
her father had left.
She didn't meet him until she was 11.

Cher was a lonely little girl.
She was looked after
by many different people.
But she had two invisible friends.
They weren't invisible children.
They were two men
called Sam and Pete.

When Cher was four years old
she went to see *Dumbo*.
From then on she wanted to be an actor
in a cartoon film!
She also sang all the time
to her Mother's records.

When Cher was 8 years old
she wanted a doll.
But she got a baby sister.
She called her Gee.
Gee was blonde like her Mother.
Cher was dark like her Father.
She always felt different.

That year they went on holiday
to Mexico.
On the way back
the guards would not let Cher pass.
They said Cher was a Mexican.
It took an hour
to make the guards see
that she was American.

The family moved yet again
when Cher was nine years old.
Stepfather No. 1 had left.
They rented a little house.
It was their first real home.
It was near the very first McDonald's.
They didn't have much money.
Sometimes they only ate crackers.
But sometimes they ate at McDonald's.

Cher went to lots of different schools
and always had problems
with English and Maths.
She made up for this
by putting on shows for her class.
She was always popular.

Cher's Mother always married poor men.
But just once
she married a very rich man.
Then Cher had a swimming pool,
a cook and a butler.
She went to school
with Frank Sinatra's little girl.
Five months later it was all over
and they were back in their little house.

3   Teenage Troubles

Cher's grandfather showed her how to drive
when she was 13.
One day she took the car
and drove her sister to Hollywood.
They had hot dogs and then drove back.

When she was 14 years old
Cher spent a night in jail.
She had taken another car.
She was always in trouble.
She was sent away to a Catholic school
because she was always falling in love.
But the girls there
were even wilder than her.

Stepfather No. 3
moved the family to New York.
Everything was different there.
It was cold
and Cher didn't know anyone.
But she soon made friends.

4 Sonny and Cher

When Cher was 16 years old
she left school and left home.
She didn't know what to do
so she went to acting classes.
She didn't think
she could be an actress
but she did want to be famous.

One day that year
she went on a date
to a Hollywood coffee shop.
She met a 28-year-old man
called Sonny Bono.
He didn't look like anyone else.
He behaved differently too.
Cher fell in love there and then.
But Sonny didn't.

Cher always wanted to be famous.

Sonny lived in the flats
next to Cher's.
They became friends.
When she was kicked out of her flat
Sonny let her move in with him.
Cher moved in with all her clothes:
one dress, two tops,
two pairs of trousers,
one coat and three pairs of shoes.
Most of them were orange.
She hates orange to this day.

When Cher's mother found out
she was angry.
This made Cher and Sonny closer
and they fell in love.

No-one else looked like Sonny and Cher.

Sonny worked for Phil Spector
in his recording studio.
He did odd jobs.
Soon Cher worked there too.

One day a backing singer was late.
Phil asked the 18-year-old Cher
to sing.
But she was too scared.
So Sonny sang with her.
It was the start of their career.
They sang back-up for a year.
The last record they sang back-up for
was one of Phil Spector's best.
It was
'You've Lost That Loving Feeling'.
It was a big hit.

Cher wanted a solo hit.
She nagged Phil until he said yes.
Cher recorded 'Ringo I Love You'.
It was terrible.
She felt that she had lost her one chance.

So Sonny and Cher
took off on their own.
They drove up and down the West Coast
singing in talent contests.
They sang other people's songs.
They wore bell bottom trousers
with stripes, spots and furs.
No-one else
looked like Sonny and Cher.

Cher's strange outfits have always brought her attention.

5 The Big Break

The USA didn't like
their looks or their music.
So Sonny and Cher
went with their new friends to England.
Their friends were the Rolling Stones.
Sonny and Cher were in the papers
from the day they got to England.

Their new single
was 'I Got You Babe'.
It was a big hit in England.
Sonny and Cher were No. 1.
The Beatles were No. 2!
For the first time
Cher had money.

When Sonny and Cher went home
they were No. 1 in the USA too.
There were 10,000 kids waiting
for them to get off the plane.

They sang on TV.
They met famous people
like Jackie Kennedy,
Elvis, Bob Dylan and the Pope.
Cher was only 20 years old.

In the next four years
they made films.
They had hit albums.
They moved into a big house.
They got married
and they had a baby.
They called her Chastity.

Cher has met lots of famous people. Here she is with the
Prince of Monaco.

6　A TV Career

In 1969 heavy metal was popular.
Nobody wanted Sonny and Cher records anymore.
They owed the Tax Man $270,000.
They were broke.
But their TV work was successful.
In 1971 they got their own show.
It was called
The Sonny and Cher Comedy Hour.
They dressed up and had a lot of fun.

In the middle
of doing their comedy show
Sonny and Cher split up.
The marriage was violent and
Cher needed her freedom.
She went out
and got her first tattoo
aged 27.

7 Making Movies

Cher went to New York
and got work on the stage.
Then a film producer saw her.
He asked her to be in his film.
Her first serious film
was called *Silkwood*.
It was about the dangers
of the nuclear power industry.

Cher was very good in *Silkwood*.
She was given a Golden Globe award
and was nominated for an Oscar in 1984.

Her next film was *Mask*.
She played a biker with a sick son.
He had an illness
that made his head grow out of shape.
Cher still raises money
to fight this illness.
Cher was superb in *Mask*.

At the end of 1974
Cher met her second husband.
His name was Greg.
They were married in Las Vegas.
10 days later she left Greg.
She didn't like the rock and roll life.
But she was pregnant.
Elijah Blue was born in 1976.

Cher was doing her own TV show.
It was called *The Cher Show*.
It was a mix of comedy and songs.
It didn't last long.

She was a single mum
with two children
and she owed money.
She had to think of something.

Cher in *The Witches of Eastwick*.

When Cher was 40
she got a star part
in *The Witches of Eastwick*.
She played one of three witches.
They summon up the devil
and then send him back!
It was a comedy.
Michelle Pfeiffer was one of
the other witches.
They had great fun making it.

Her other film that year
was *Moonstruck*.
She plays a woman
who is engaged to one man
but she falls in love with his younger brother.
Cher was so good in *Moonstruck*
that she won an Oscar for it, in 1988.

Cher in the hit film, *Mermaids*.

Cher had two hits with her next film.
It was called *Mermaids*.
One was the film itself.
Cher plays Mrs Flax.
In the film
she is Christina Ricci's crazy mum.
Mrs Flax is just like Cher's own mother.

The other hit
was 'The Shoop Shoop Song'
from the film.

8   Recent Times

Cher got her dark looks
from her Armenian father.
In 1993 she went to Armenia.
They had a big earthquake in 1988.
Cher took the people
food, clothes and toys.
She said,
'It was the only place I'd ever been
where everyone looked like me.'
She will always remember that trip.

1998 was a year of ups and downs for Cher.
She finished writing a book.
It was called *The First Time*
and it was about her life.
Then in January, Sonny died.
Cher was in England.
She was going to open the Harrods' sale.
She flew back to LA for the funeral.
The loss was hard for Cher.
She cried for a long time.

Cher's film success meant that she was often at the Oscars.

At the end of 1998
Cher's single 'Believe' came out.
It was the biggest selling single
of the year.
It was the best-selling song
by a woman in the UK ever!
She was also
the oldest woman to have a No. 1 hit.
'Believe' sold 1.7 million copies.

Over the years
Cher has had surgery to
change her looks.
Perhaps this is why she
still seems so young.
But perhaps she would still be
beautiful anyway.

In January 1999
Cher came back to England.
This time she did open the Harrods' sale!

Cher at the Brit Awards in 1999. In 1998 Cher had the biggest selling single of the year.

In 2000 Cher recorded
her second Greatest Hits album.
Then she started a film
with Jennifer Aniston.
They play a pair of con-artists
who are mother and daughter.

Cher has had at least two careers!
It seems like she will go on forever.
She is a world-class survivor.